"Leonardini's manuscript simple explanations, he ge of *Toxic Shame* and the destructive power it has on one's psyche and spiritual life. For those who are incarcerated in prisons of brick and mortar or of their own minds, Leonardini opens the way for a deeper liberation from the wounds of *Toxic Shame* through contemplative practice and deep compassionate listening. His work is no doubt a timely and transformational contribution to the spiritual growth of inmates who struggle to come to terms with their own self-worth and the realization that they are indeed lovable."

– Fr. Vincent Pizzuto, PhD,
Teacher and Author of *Contemplating Christ:
The Gospels and the Interior Life.*

The great "slayer of the soul." This is what Ray Leonardini aptly calls "toxic shame." In this, his latest contribution, Leonardini has penned a precious gift: he gives a voice to those who have no voice. By allowing prisoners to speak of their own shame we hear in their voices echoes of our own. These voices and echoes of voices reveals the one Great Silence whose voice rings out, "My love is stronger than your shame."

– Martin Laird, O.S.A.
Lecturer, Retreat Director, and Author of *An Ocean of Light.*

"Ray Leonardini's work on toxic shame is a welcome addition to the contemplative literature. Using practical examples drawn from his work with prisoners, he explores how this destructive dynamic operates in the lives of traumatized individuals and the healing that comes when it is addressed in the context of a contemplative group. In my experience, the pattern is endemic to many other groups and populations, including the recovery community, and his method bears study for use in other settings."

– John Ensign, PhD,
Jungian Analyst and Retreat Director.

"Ray Leonardini, by addressing the pain of toxic shame, has made a valuable contribution that helps bring incarcerated men and women from the bondage of darkness, into the light of healing. Using examples anyone can relate to, he exposes how uninformed, negative behaviors on the part of so-called "good" people – parents, teachers, neighbors and friends - have the potential to leave life-wounding results that can only be dispensed with by inner listening, trust, honesty and the development (or rediscovery) of one's faith. This work is consistent with our experience of recovery at its best."

– Judith Stevens,
Founder and Manager, The Prison Outreach Program,
Edgar Cayce's Association for Research
and Enlightenment (A.R.E.)Inc.

"Chaplain Ray Leonardini has taken on a very difficult issue, toxic shame, with the loving compassion that he brings to all of his work. His kindhearted energy invites readers to feel safe and loved while working with a triggering topic."

– Catherine Dumas
Executive Director, Human Kindness Foundation.

"I have honestly never seen this topic addressed before in the context of prison work. It's much needed. It is truly amazing that many incarcerated folks, given the chance, are able to go into their shame without seeming to want to hide even when they hear their own words said out loud. After 25 years of doing this, I believe that of all human beings those who have been in prison have a handle on some of these processes in ways that the rest of us do not have. We can learn much from them."

– Gloria Kempton
Prison volunteer and teacher in
Prisons and Jails for over 25 years.

"Through years of interacting with prisoners and teaching Centering Prayer, Leonardini has masterfully aligned both the spiritual and psychological in affecting inner healing and in beginning the journey into recovery. His teaching of "toxic shame" in a prison environment that only reinforces personal shame has enabled prisoners to be led to a safe place within themselves. Here, they trust enough to discover and name their unspoken pain. The journey now begins in earnest to dismantle the barriers of a lifetime where, in prayerful centering, these are held, named and slowly released. This process, in turn, effects a slow but gentle "rebirth" as they learn to claim their sacred humanity buried beneath so much shame and unresolved pain."

– **Sister Catherine Marie Bazar, O.P.**
Volunteer Chaplain for 25 years, Los Angeles County Jail, 'The Tombs'.

ALSO BY RAY LEONARDINI

Finding God Within:
Contemplative Prayers for Prisoners

I only wish I had this guidance and advice when I was a jail chaplain for fourteen years. You do not need to fly by the seat of your pants anymore! When you have access to a man as patient and experienced as Ray Leonardini, you would be wise to let him guide you–in one of the least supported and yet most needed ministries of Christianity.

– **Fr. Richard Rohr, O.F.M.**, Center for Action and Contemplation; author, *Breathing under Water.*

TOXIC SHAME and CONTEMPLATIVE PRAYER

From Hiding to Healing

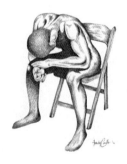

Ray Leonardini
Prison Contemplative Fellowship

Copyright © 2019 Ray Leonardini

All rights reserved. No part of this book may be reproduced, stored in a retrieval system, or transmitted in any form or by any means, electronic, mechanical, photocopying, recording, or otherwise without written permission of Prison Contemplative Fellowship.

For additional copies, free to prisoners, please write to:
Prison Contemplative Fellowship
P.O. Box 1086
Folsom, CA 95763-1086
USPCF.org
email: office@USPCF.org

Printed in the United States

Names: Ray Leonardini, author
Title: Toxic Shame and Contemplative Prayer: From Hiding to Healing

ISBN 9780996916646

Prison Contemplative Fellowship is a community of prisoners, chaplains, and volunteers who practice a form of Christian silent prayer called centering prayer. It is a fellowship that recognizes our individuality and celebrates our unique relationship with the Divine.

The symbol of the Cross, adapted for prisoners, points to the key to our freedom. We acknowledge that it is through the mysterious transformation of our suffering in centering prayer that brings the vital change we deeply desire.

This work is dedicated to
incarcerated men and women who
over the years had the courage
to recognize and talk about their
own toxic shame, and to those not
in prison who recognize their own
shame and encouraged me to
publish this essay.

TABLE OF CONTENTS

Preface xvi
Part One: *The Soul Slayer* 1
    1. Experiencing Toxic Shame
    2. Recognizing Toxic Shame
    3. The Unthinkable
    4. Don't Tell Anyone
    5. Shame in the School Yard
    6. Disciplinary Shaming
    7. Crossing the Great Divide
    8. The Aftermath of Sexual Assault
    9. Recovering a Sense of Self in a World of Shame

Interlude: *Prisoners In Their Own Voice* 17
Part Two: *The Way Out of Our Shame* 21
    1. Learn How to Listen. Start with Yourself
    2. Find One Person to Trust
    3. Build a Home for Your Shame
    4. Starting an Honest Relationship with God
    5. Learning Intimacy with God
    6. The Prodigal Son. Luke 15:11-32
    7. Intimacy with a Father

Conclusion 37
Endnotes 39
Appendices 41
    A. A simple way to do centering prayer
    B. Guidelines for a centering prayer circle
Resources 45

PREFACE

Ray Leonardini's piece on toxic shame takes on the difficult process of discovering our own shame as we reflect on shame in incarcerated people. It is difficult because this type of shame is hidden deep in our unconscious and because its origins lie in moments of deep personal pain. To approach this shame Leonardini suggests becoming silent enough through a contemplative practice like centering prayer. Sooner or later, but inevitably, the unconscious will begin to unload, that is, bring into consciousness things previously hidden. This unloading allows us to experience our false self, the ways we remain self-centered and manipulate reality rather than seeing what is actually there. As we begin to recognize the variety of roles and dodges that embody our false self, a deeper sense of shame begins to be felt. Leonardini likens the emergence of this second [or deeper] shame as coming to a Great Divide—the Rockies or the Mississippi River that one has to traverse to get from here (West Coast) to there (East Coast). Are we going to stop or are we going to continue forward on this long journey into night? Since this is an essential part of the spiritual path, the reader should be alerted that this new unloading will happen.

Leonardini rightly points out that centering prayer group facilitators in prisons and jails can and should encourage the sharing of this vital personal material in a prayer group. People in contemplative prayer groups in prisons as described in his previous books, particularly *Finding God Within*: Contemplative Prayer for Prisoners, have learned to sit with silence, and allow to arise whatever arises. Practitioners call this process divine therapy. And so group members are better prepared to allow someone to disclose a secret shame from childhood, a shame that shaped and disrupted that person's whole life and being. While listening respectfully, such a disclosure can also open a window into listeners' own deeply repressed toxic shame. This process resonates and invites them to begin to look at their own deeply buried shame. This monograph is not an easy, comfortable read for the casual reader. It points to a challenging encounter with deep personal realities that often hold us back from our sense of God's presence and our God-given destiny. As Part Two describes, there is a way out of this personal pain. Those with a contemplative prayer practice will recognize the stages of health and spiritual growth. First awareness, then holding still with the pain, finally the gradual integration into Self and a new sense of connection with the Divine.

Not an easy path, but one well worth taking.

– Tim O'Connell, Ph.D

Dr. Tim O'Connell, is a clinical psychologist and long-term meditator. He is also a Certified Holotropic Breathwork trainer.

PART ONE

The Soul Slayer

Over years of teaching and practicing contemplative prayer in prisons, I have come to recognize the pervasive and destructive reality of toxic shame. Guilt is the feeling we have when we have done something we consider to be wrong. Shame is how we feel about who we are because of what we have done. What is called "Toxic Shame" is in a different category. It is not the rightful shame one feels when they know they have done something wrong. Rather, it is the unconscious shame that hides in the deep psyche. This shame says: I am wrong. It is called toxic shame because it functions as a silent master emotion that unconsciously, and beyond the reach of ordinary awareness, seeps into and poisons every feeling we have about ourselves.[1] I have witnessed repeatedly in prison groups toxic shame as the most daunting obstacle to people seeking healing transformation through a contemplative practice. In my experience this toxic shame, not the shame associated with a crime, is a silent killer, so dangerous to the psyche, so threatening to one's intimate sense of one's self, that it effectively cuts the person off from the deepest part of themselves where they encounter God.

I have also seen how contemplative prayer offers a near miraculous antidote to toxic shame. If toxic shame is allowed into consciousness in the safe context of a contemplative prayer group, it can facilitate remarkable transformation and new-found personal freedom.

Since institutional dehumanization in prisons and jails is the norm, toxic shame among people who are incarcerated is pervasive and invisible, hard to bear, and even harder to talk about. I decided to write this monograph on toxic shame to raise awareness around this topic so detrimental to the inner life. It comes out indirectly in self-judgments: 'I feel like a complete phony' or 'I feel like God is disgusted with me.' Daily life in a high security prison requires vigilance and self-protection for survival, so uncovering toxic shame in a group context requires facing difficult emotions and subtle movements of the soul. Acknowledging it openly can seem nearly impossible.

The dominant role toxic shame plays in prison life is not well-known and can easily be missed.[2] But recognizing shame and helping people reflect on its effects makes a major difference to them. Introductory workshops for centering prayer, even those in a prison context, tend not to address the negative power of toxic shame. Beginners in centering prayer hear about 'unloading the unconscious' along with 'afflictive emotions,' like anger, resentments, jealousy, and so forth. Rarely is shame itself a topic. Toxic shame as a master emotion that fuels our inmost fear is never discussed. Ignoring toxic shame is not unique to Centering Prayer Workshops. Delving into deeply buried matters of personal history to get to the source of toxic shame is a messy, confusing, and discouraging experience. As a result, despite the heart-opening work of those who facilitate centering prayer in prisons, the paralyzing effect of toxic shame often remains hidden. Sequestered in the deep unconscious, and protected by well-developed defense mechanisms, it continues to poison the person's sense of self, while controlling motives and actions. Yet, mysteriously, uncovering toxic shame in the context of contemplative prayer offers existential hope and healing beyond any reasonable expectation.

Experiencing Toxic Shame

Though it may seem unfair, those wounded by shame often take entire responsibility for the event that triggered it (see Andrew's story below). When we have been lured or pressured into encounters that leave us ashamed, many of us do not recognize our own relative innocence and cannot give ourselves the benefit of the doubt. Shame disables and distorts a healthy, balanced view of ourselves. For many of us, toxic shame makes us feel as if we do not have the right to exist. It is a razor to the soul that cuts into the psyche so insidiously the individual is unaware he or she may be bleeding to death.

The strategies we devise for protecting ourselves from the pain of toxic shame are a core factor in the development of a false self as we try to avoid the overwhelming feeling of shame at any cost. Many people discover that their shame-based behaviors started early in life, although they had long-forgotten, or repressed the triggering incidents. Bessel Van Der Kolk, MD, puts it this way:

> When your caregivers turn on you, you have to find alternative ways to deal with feeling scared, angry, or frustrated. Managing your terror all by yourself gives rise to another set of problems: dissociation, despair, addiction, a chronic sense of panic, and relationships that are marked by alienation, disconnection, and explosions. *Patients with these histories rarely make connection between what happened to them long ago and how they currently feel and behave.* Everything just seems unmanageable.[3]

As a result, incarcerated people, like the rest of us, do not know how to access their own spiritual healing powers.

Depth psychologists, like Carl Jung, tell us that toxic shame is passed on from generation to generation. It is as if toxic shame is carried in the genes. Marriages can be derailed through partners' failure to recognize the shame they carry.

Not surprisingly, therefore, a major outcome of toxic shame is an inability to experience intimacy. As it is more and more deeply internalized, it becomes the driving force behind an increasing sense of isolation and abandonment. It may take the better part of a lifetime to become aware of shame and talk about it.

Just as shame is an obstacle to human intimacy, it is also a block in contemplative prayer practice, the major goal of which is *intimacy with God*.[4] How can we freely accept the invitation to intimacy with the Divine if our fundamental human affections are blunted by personal shame? How can we take in the love of God if we experience ourselves to be unlovable and incapable of intimacy?

Shame is how we feel about who we are because of what we have done… "Toxic Shame" is the unconscious shame that hides in the deep psyche. This shame says: I am wrong.

Recognizing Toxic Shame

Discovering the impact of toxic shame, particularly early-onset toxic shame, is not a left-brain experience. We cannot "figure out" the shaming experience because, most of the time, we have no conscious memory of it. Yet, as I have sat in contemplative prayer with hundreds of groups in prisons, listened to stories of people who lived in solitary confinement, and watched the slow emergence of long-repressed material, I have seen how recognition of early childhood trauma leads to awareness of toxic shame.

The normal pattern of contemplative prayer groups at Folsom Prison begins with centering prayer, then moves to various topics related to the spiritual journey. Early on the subject of the false self enters discussions. We begin to recognize how we have adopted various roles to satisfy parental and group expectations. Only after some familiarity with notions of the false self, and what Thomas Keating calls the unloading of the unconscious, can the topic of shame be introduced. Now we are appropriately in the arena of the spiritual view of divine therapy, an interpersonal therapy that invites the Divine into the picture. Only at that point is it possible to find the pathway into early childhood trauma and shaming experiences.

However, I am encouraged by the fact that if only one person in the group has the courage to talk about such early childhood experiences, it opens similar permission for everyone in the group. One person's painful articulation of shame can open the listeners to their own internal narratives and unveils their own shame. They may not talk about it immediately, but they begin to recognize their own toxic shame. Ironically, this new consciousness of shame, this new internal awareness, can also happen to those in solitary confinement with a contemplative prayer practice.

In the stories that follow, we will see how the members of a particular group come to recognize their own shame because one brave soul has first admitted to their own. Each of these stories was shared in a group of incarcerated people. Each of the stories had a dramatic impact on the group and brought it closer in a palpable way. In my observation, this movement toward solidarity and openness came not simply from compassion for the speaker, but from the way the speaker opened for each listener a window into his own silent shame. In other words, very often the group felt the solidarity and compassion while the speaker, in the midst of his story, oftentimes still felt alienated and shamed.

The Unthinkable

When I was first in elementary school, maybe first or second grade, I went into the bathroom. In there was an older kid, maybe fifth grade. Whatever he was doing, he didn't want me in there. He grabbed me and forced me to put my hands into a full toilet bowl and squish the material in the bowl.

I don't remember much after that except that I was able to wash my hands before I went back into the classroom. But, **I didn't tell anyone***. It has taken me nearly 60 years to be able to allow myself to sit in silence, without judgment, with this pain. Only after this sitting in silence, could I begin to speak about it. Centering prayer has taught me that the more I sit in the pain, the less I hurt, the less I hurt, the more I feel, and the more I experience the release of my shame. During these many years I didn't recognize how desperately I tried to avoid remembering this experience of total helplessness. I could not feel my shame or even think about the incident. If the slightest hint of the feeling of total helplessness ever emerged, I thought I'd rather die, or kill someone, than feel that feeling. The core of the shame, I know now, however irrational, was the constant self-reproach:* **how could I let this happen to me without fighting back?**

Somewhere deep inside I unconsciously resolved that I was not going to allow myself to ever feel my degrading powerlessness ever again! I can see now it directed much of my rage all through my life. It's like nothing that anyone outside of me, police or guards, could do to me would match my own personal shame.

- Andrew

Don't Tell Anyone

Many of the complicated emotions that emerge from our depths when we start our spiritual journeys in earnest are familiar. Anger, jealousy, humiliation, fear, resentment, and so forth, are easily recognizable, though painful. Even if we choose not to deal with them, and continue to repress them, listening to other people's stories evoke these feelings, and we recognize them in ourselves.

This is not true of toxic shame. Shame is an experience of an entirely different order. We can have experiences of anger and resentment. We are shame. It is as if some part of our being is fundamentally wrong. It is not that we did something wrong, we are wrong. The fact that we can remain for years unaware of our buried shame suggests that as we keep shameful experiences secret, we stop acknowledging them to ourselves. We not only deny to others our dreadful experience as a kid, we even stop telling ourselves. It seems contradictory that even though the toxic shame is buried in our unconscious, removed from our conscious sense of self, it continues to influence our behavior in a subterranean way. But depth psychologists tell us that such is the reality of the unconscious. If any event even remotely triggered Andrew's unconscious pain, he just knew he 'would rather die or kill someone' than feel that feeling again. Shame like this functions like a foul odor you can smell, but cannot determine the source.

Blotting out shameful experiences makes sense when we understand that the psyche is protecting us by shutting down our memory of the event. So as Andrew grew older, and he developed a contemplative prayer practice, he was ready to look at this toxic shame.

As I sit in silence more things come and go. The more I let go, the less that binds me. The silence of centering prayer transforms my life without major effort.[5]

As Andrew's ability to take a wider view of his life increased, the repression of this trauma receded. As it emerged into his awareness, his contemplative prayer practice allowed him to sit still with it.

Shame in the School Yard

It was 3:15 on a Friday afternoon and school was just getting out. All the kids were running around, talking, laughing, and getting in the last bit of play for the week. I too was with my friends, walking to the front of the school to get on the bus as we usually did. All we could do was laugh and talk about what we would do over the weekend.

As I turned around the corner approaching the front of the school I was quickly snatched up by someone. I noticed the look of shock on my friends' faces. As I turned to see who it was, I realized it was my father. When the first open hand across my butt came I didn't understand. When the second strike came I noticed ten thousand eyes peering down on me. With the third I saw the jeers. With the fourth they were pointing. And finally, with the fifth blow I saw even the teachers laughing.

I have no idea whether these people were really laughing at me or not. But that is exactly what I saw. **I felt their eyes staring at me** *as my father dragged me off to the car that afternoon. And, as he drove me home for the rest of my punishment, all I could think of was what would be said all weekend long. And more importantly, who would laugh when I returned to school the following Monday?*

I was placed on restriction that day, unable to leave my room: a prison within itself. As I sat there counting the hours, all I could think about was the faces. With each imagined thought my heart raced, my breath shortened. I could not stop the thoughts from coming. I wondered what I should do in the event someone mocked me on Monday. Should I accept the taunts? Should I verbally check my tormentors? Or should I lash out to the fullest and fight? All these thoughts raced along in my head. And up to that moment, I had no idea what my response would be.

When I returned to school that Monday, I was on eggshells. "His friends' eyes caused more shame than his father's hand. It is central to his pain." *I walked with my head down, defeated by all who even thought to say something. People were quiet for the most part, but I just 'knew' that as I passed they were saying: "Hey, that's the guy whose dad whooped him Friday."* **I felt their stares for days.** *All the way up till something more pressing occurred in the school, taking the eye of mockery off me.*

– Lamar

Disciplinary Shaming

Shame enters the psyche through a side door. Reading Lamar's story, we might rationally think that the hard part for him was receiving the beating. But that appears not to be the case. The hard shaming part for him was being seen by his friends receiving the beating. It is as if their eyes were worse than his father's hands.

Their witnessing his humiliation was the deep penetrating wound. It shattered his self-image. His dad was probably not trying to shame him those many years ago. It is unlikely that he chose to discipline his son in public because he wanted his son's friends to see his humiliation. He probably thought he was just delivering fair punishment for some misbehavior. But shame him he did.

We can easily miss the critical importance of *being seen* in the disciplinary shaming of Lamar. Seeing and allowing ourselves to be seen, by our self first, then by God, is integral to unraveling the mystery of toxic shame. Understanding its role, as we will see below, is essential to defeating this great slayer of the soul.

Ordinary reasoning cannot get to the bottom of our shame. We must find other ways to access this deep pain. Transpersonal psychology tells us that transformative change (i.e., change that reaches our most personally held view of our self) comes only through experiences that go beyond the reach of our usual self talk. Deep and prolonged suffering, dreams, grief, deep love, movies that awaken unexpected feelings, stirring music can help us access this vulnerable part of ourselves. This makes sense because our habitual thinking simply reruns the destructive narrative loop. This perhaps is the only place where people in prison may have an advantage on the spiritual journey, if one can consider any kind of suffering to be an advantage. Their unconscious and persistent suffering is long-term. In over 10 years working with people in prisons, I have heard a majority of them who join contemplative prayer sessions describe terrifying experiences of shame apparently deliberately inflicted by a parent or guardian.

When people are able to recall these painful memories, they begin to restructure their awareness of their experience. Seemingly out of nowhere, they can begin to understand their personal sense of alienation and separation from their innermost self. They can begin to recognize shame as the source of their anger in a way they never could prior to this new opening. It does restructure the stories they tell themselves about themselves. Lamar can now understand in a profoundly new way how his friends staring at him was repressed into his unconscious, waiting for a time when he could safely remember it. It was simply too hard to bear when he was a kid.

The hard shaming part for him was being seen by his friends receiving the beating. It is as if their eyes were worse than his father's hands.

Crossing the Great Divide

Introducing someone to a receptive contemplative practice like centering prayer without telling them that it is likely to unearth buried shame and trauma is like giving someone a map of a route from the West Coast to the East Coast that does not indicate they will be crossing the Rocky Mountains or the Mississippi River. If you are forewarned of the emergence of painful difficulties, you feel more prepared and are not blindsided when they emerge. It is not uncommon to hear someone say, in a group dealing with shame, 'I haven't thought about that experience in 40 years.'

Shame often seems insurmountable; an impossible barrier to continuing the spiritual journey. However, as we detach from thoughts we recognize shame is an illusion. We begin to see from a new perspective and with a greater detachment, the shaming experience that insinuates the lie: "I am fatally flawed, and fundamentally a bad person." The shame we are addressing in these challenging moments is the toxic shame lodged in the depths of our soul. We are not dealing with the appropriate shame we feel when we have knowingly violated our own sense of right action. Early childhood shame is toxic to our most intimate notion of self. This shame wraps itself like a tumor around vital organs. It is so closely connected to our habits of mind and behavior that we can easily fail to recognize its presence.

'Crossing the Great Divide,' that is, getting to the place where we can peer into the depths of our self, starts with willingness to 'go through' our most personal experiences of this shame. Practitioners of silent meditation like contemplative prayer have an advantage here. It is only by resisting our inclination to run and hide from our shame that healing begins. We have to experience the thing we most wish not to experience even as we come to see that to flee it is even worse. The gift of contemplative prayer is the capacity to witness the raw parts of our self without judgment and self-loathing. This type of witnessing can happen when holding still in the gaze of the Divine. As we shall see, contemplative prayer opens us to the healing available to us in the contemplative moment.

The Aftermath of Sexual Assault

I came to a low point in my life around my late teens, early adult years. On an evening shortly after my twentieth birthday I was in a fight that quickly became extremely violent, with multiple attackers. During the altercation I was sexually assaulted. (It's difficult for me to even write about this 20 years later.) When the fight was over I felt my powerlessness and could only think that it could have been worse. When I saw one of my assailants a week or so later, I apologized! Not too long afterwards I remember I was lying on my back writhing with feelings of intense paralysis, anxiety, and self-loathing. WHY DID I APOLOGIZE? I had no answer. I decided that the world was going to pay for what it had done to me. I felt expelled from the Garden.

Now twenty years later I'm sitting in prison trying to understand the difficulty of that part of my life and the reality of a trauma experienced and a shame unprocessed. Trauma and shame locked me into a rigid, polarized view of reality: good vs. evil, innocence vs. guilt, ME vs. YOU. A world view of black and white with no center, no grey areas where human beings discover themselves and each other.

My meditation practice has helped me to see that there is no place other than this place, this moment. As Thomas Merton once wrote: "The desert becomes a paradise when it is accepted for the desert that it is." My life is no longer about overcoming my trauma and shame but consenting to the experiences of my life in the now, here. Through grace I realize that God meets me in this place I am in. God comes to me in this place where I am. Now. Here.

– Josh

Recovering a Sense of Self in a World of Shame

Few people talk about how you get out of shame. Reputable psychologists and therapists acknowledge their own flight from personal experiences of shame. It seems as though the more shame we have, the deeper we go into our caves. We do not want anyone to see it. We put a stone in front of our cave, so no one can get in and we cannot get out.

Twenty years ago, I wrote a book on all the troubling places the soul might visit in this long and unsteady journey we call our life. 'Swamplands of the Soul' describes such marshy zones as depression, guilt, anxiety, loss, addiction, betrayal, and many other dreary visitations. After it was published one reader wrote to me and said: "Why did you not include shame?" "Huh," I thought, "why didn't I? It is so obvious." I thought a long time on that question and am still puzzling over it these many years later when I tell myself I really ought to know better. I finally concluded that, dismal as those other places were, I had a special resistance to writing about shame and managed to 'forget' it in the list on my Hades Mystery Tour.[6]

Prisoners can admit to many kinds of personal failure. But toxic shame is on a different level. On their own, people in prison don't go to that level, ever. They have spent a lifetime avoiding and denying the trauma that is often the root of shame. [7]

This makes sense when one understands how early childhood trauma shapes the psyche of a young person. They are not equipped to integrate these soul-searing wounds into consciousness. The survival response is to bury them in the deepest part of the unconscious.

Why did I apologize?

Prisoners In Their Own Voice

This was written for me!
– Anonymous

"The more I'm able to sit still with the pain of toxic shame, the less the painful ache is tied to specific memories. For me, I'm triggered by the memories. As I sit in the silence with the ache, I seem to find a way through the pain. In some way it becomes more manageable."

– **Ket 'B' Vichitvongsa**

"When I turn my shame inside out it is rage. Rage is anger mixed with hatred. If triggered anything horrible is possible. Before centering prayer toxic shame mines were buried and hidden everywhere. I could explode without warning. For me, centering prayer is like a mine detector. If I feel something getting too close, I can stop and breathe. I go into the spaciousness of silence to deactivate the trauma. Before I learned this approach to feelings of shame, I thought my responsibility was to accept blame and shame. Now I find that I can respond better to the triggering event before the need to act."

– **Lawrence Hamilton**

"I love this stuff. This should be read by everyone not just prisoners. We all know that our life is full of critical 'moments,' some are full of shame, some are full of satisfaction. What I've come to understand is that the real value for all of these moments, especially here with shame, is to honor and understand them because they can make us into the people we were born to be."

– **Rob Crutchlow**

"Centering Prayer allows me to deal with all those events and memories that I have chosen to avoid, especially the painful and shameful ones, I find as I deal with them, little by little, they lose their power over me."

– Daniel Delgado

"For many years, I have felt, not like I made a mistake, but that I am a mistake. This feeling was so deep in me I didn't know it was a feeling. It was the state of my mind. I have come to recognize my experience of toxic shame in the last couple of years and now realize that we all suffer from shame in some form or another. Most former prisoners I meet confuse shame and guilt. Guilt: I made a mistake. Shame: I am the mistake. The work done by Ray Leonardini and Prison Contemplative Fellowship and prison contemplative prayer groups really helps to clarify and free us to separate who we are from what's been done to us, or what we've done."

– Greg Gibson

PART TWO

The Way Out of Our Shame

Psychologists agree that the way out of toxic shame, once it emerges from the repressed unconscious, is to externalize the trauma by confiding in one individual about one's sense of soul-loathing -- the sense that we have lost our right to exist. Healing begins as we allow ourselves to come out of hiding, allowing ourselves to leave the cave, and trust someone enough to let them see our pain. While at first glance finding one person to whom one can reveal their shame may sound relatively simple, it is not at all the case in a prison context. The reason for this complexity has less to do with the trustworthiness of people who are locked up together, and more to do with the psychological remoteness of toxic shame itself. Thus, the importance of group experiences of contemplative prayer where toxic shame is an agreed-upon topic. The centering prayer group can be led to this point if the facilitator maps the spiritual journey of divine therapy from the unloading of the unconscious, to the discovery of the false self that brings the group to the door of shame. At this door of shame, the facilitator can present case studies as those presented above that create the arena for triggering personal experiences of shame.

The group takes it from there. I have never seen it fail. It is as if the group creates the energy out of which emerge personal anecdotes of toxic shame.

The unique setting of a centering prayer group provides a safe place to begin this talk. We do not underestimate the courage required to talk about the experience of toxic shame. This is especially true in a jail or penitentiary where one must never disclose a personal weakness: to do so would be to risk personal safety. Josh's ability to "hold" the penetrating question: Why did I apologize? allowed him to wait for a time of safety that gradually gave him a path to healing. It also allowed him to share his experience in a centering prayer group.

Healing begins as we allow ourselves to come out of hiding, allowing ourselves to leave the cave, and trust someone enough to let them see our pain.

Learn How to Listen
Start With Yourself

Learning to listen is key to a personal relationship as well as the development of a safe group. Whether listening alone or in a group, the listening person provides a home, a place to return to and be accepted, a place where the speaker may come safely with all his or her hopes for being known and understood. Real listening, non-anxious listening, means that the hearer is not mentally preparing a response as the speaker talks. It means that the listener is totally present, in the present moment, to the words of the speaker. Listening of this kind is not self-protective; a good listener does not try to shut down or divert the speaker because the listener cannot handle the speaker's pain. This is particularly effective in a group. Contemplative groups have an advantage here because the members are not afraid of group silence, which is often the most appropriate response to a story of toxic shame.

Hospice workers, for example, will tell you that non-anxious listening is an absolute requirement for engaging a dying person. After all, what is there to say to someone who knows they are dying? Sentiments like, "It's OK," or "You're going to be just fine," does not make any sense. It is the silence itself that is powerful, not the superficial words we use to fill the silence. So too as we witness our own and another's shame.

This capacity to listen, in my experience, is directly related to the capacity to be comfortable with silence. If silence is difficult to maintain, non-anxious listening will be nearly impossible.

Ironically for contemplative prayer practitioners this kind of listening, this ease with silence, is integral to a contemplative practice. The first lessons in centering prayer deal with the ebb and flow of 'thoughts,' a generic term for anything that pops into awareness during the prayer time. We are taught to let them come and go and not react to whatever emerges. Silent listening begins with our self each time we sit for prayer.

Our ability to sit in silence with our own shame and trauma as it buffets our awareness is perfect practice for non-anxious listening. If we cannot sit still, if we must distract our self from the moments of pain that emerge in our own prayer practice, there is little likelihood we will be able to sit still with another person's story of shame.

Find One Person to Trust

Written and unwritten rules in jails and penitentiaries make trust difficult. Difficulty with trust is one of the reasons gangs are rampant in penal institutions. In prison or jail, people want to know whom they can trust. But the pursuit of trust is more than political, it is human. It comes from our need to be heard, seen, and accepted. In the scheme of centering prayer's divine therapy, our early instinctual needs for 'affection and esteem' are the biological foundation for the development of trust. If early parental or guardian relationships are inadequate, even without intentional mistreatment, our appropriate need for affection and self-esteem is never satisfied. Attachment Theory tells us that these children will always experience significant problems with personal relationships and find trust to be often out of reach.

Although this seems like a death sentence for a young person, particularly when significant traumas are identified, I have witnessed, time and again in contemplative prayer groups, the ability of a person with early childhood trauma to beat the odds by recognizing and describing their toxic shame. The group holds still listening to stories of parental homicide and abuse as the speaker comes to terms with it in a realistic and remarkably healthy way.

I have witnessed and met many of these children of grace in our contemplative prayer groups. The compassion and kindness toward people that is emerging in their centering prayer practice now is given to one's self.

Build a Home for Your Shame

The simple practice in centering prayer of letting go of thoughts, that is, not resisting and not retaining the thoughts and feelings that emerge during prayer, is a deeply transformative practice. As one psychiatrist aptly put it: "Trauma (and shame) become sufferable, even illuminating when there is a relational home to hold it in. Without this, it is simply too much to bear."[8]

As we sit with our shame, and allow the pain of it to emerge, we give ourselves what we needed in the first place—a nonjudgmental understanding presence, a 'home,' to comfort us. Creating this home gives us the safe space we need, and appreciation for the subtleties of another's shame, to sit in non-anxious presence and become the friend the speaker truly needs.

For some, this notion of creating a "home" for the shame appears to be at odds with the hope of dissolving or dispelling the shame. This touches one of the most subtle, even mysterious attributes of contemplative prayer: *healing* shame by holding still with it. It reminds me of the "unmanageable" part of the first step in the Twelve Steps. By the act of acknowledging that life is unmanageable because of our addiction, we somehow begin the process of making it manageable. In centering prayer, holding still in silence is allowing God to gaze upon us, love us as always from all eternity since our moment of creation. In this intimacy of eternal love, without words, even without thoughts, we are brought back to our most personal self. Practitioners get this experience even though they are rarely able to describe it in words. What they notice is that each time the shaming experience emerges into their awareness (in or outside of contemplation) its searing intensity softens a bit, goes from level 10 to level 9. This softening allows the experience to emerge more fully into awareness. Deeper understanding of one's self continues to unfold in healing ways. This healing experience happens as well for the *listener in a centering prayer group* because their own silence in the group contributes to the sense of "home" for the speaker.

Starting an Honest Relationship with God

From the perspective of the spiritual journey, the way out of toxic shame is allowing God to 'see' us, allowing God to gaze on us. Remember Lamar's story? His shame was rooted in his knowing that his classmates were *looking at him*. His shame is like Adam and Eve's when they hid in their nakedness because they didn't want God to 'see' them.

> *Toward evening they heard the Lord God walking about in the garden, so they hid themselves among the trees. The Lord God called to Adam, "Where are you?" He replied, "I heard you, so I hid. I was afraid because I was naked."*
> – Genesis 3:8-10

If we are honest with ourselves, coming out of hiding and allowing God to see us can be as difficult and perilous as confiding in another human being about the pain of our toxic shame.

But we must find a way to start. The first step of healing begins when we can acknowledge, if only to ourselves, our sense of estrangement from God and consider the *possibility* of a different relationship with a God who sees us and loves us. If we feel estranged or alienated from ourselves, we will feel something similar toward God.

Our assessment of our relationship with God is more complicated as God is as much a mystery to our deeper selves as we are to ourselves. We have both a concept of God and an operative *emotional image* of God. The concept of God may be debated by philosophers and theologians. This may be the God we talk about if asked whether we believe. The God who touches us at an emotional level has much more to do with how we feel about *ourselves*. Studies have found that belief in a wrathful God is connected to our sense of loneliness. The greater the loneliness, the more likely it is that we see God as wrathful. Our tendency to project onto other people those parts of our self we find unattractive is also at work in our relationship with God.[9]

I often hear people in prison say: *'I feel that God is disappointed with me,'* or *'I feel guilty all the time when I think of God.' 'I don't ask God for anything because I've screwed up so much.'* These are the words of loneliness, isolation and shame, although they are rarely treated as such. Too often they are treated by professional religious people as preliminaries to begging God for forgiveness of all the 'bad' things done in one's life, and the promise of living a reformed life. Asking for forgiveness may be appropriate, but it does not help one's sense of original shame. We are taught about the necessity of asking for forgiveness. We are never taught about the self-destructive impacts of toxic shame. Evaluating how I honestly feel about myself in relationships truly helps me to discover what my actual relationship with God is.

Many of us rely on the initiative of God to heal the wounds of our shame. We have been taught this and believe this to be true. We are taught that if we pray hard enough, plead with God long enough, then the relationship will prosper. This is true as far as it goes, but, honestly, it doesn't go very far when we look at the depths of our own shame. A life-long pattern of shame-based decisions in all our relationships can easily overwhelm our intentions to revise our unhealthy image of God. Where do we go from here? Enter the spiritual dynamics of contemplative prayer and nondual awareness.

Learning Intimacy with God

Psychological healing from toxic shame begins when we allow it into our awareness and share it with one person, or a small contemplative group. Similarly, spiritual healing begins as we find our 'home' in God. For many incarcerated people even the thought of an intimate relationship with the Divine is nearly impossible to consider. Yet understanding our own spiritual journey, in the context of our contemplative prayer practice, allows us to see that changing our relationship with God is possible. As we sit in silence, we discover a *personal guidance* system inside, with its own gravitational draw toward the Divine.

It works like this: as we 'hold' the shame that emerges on its own, without trying to dump it or cling to it, our perception of the shame starts to shift on its own. Because this shift is outside of our normal cognitive awareness, and separate from any movement of will power, we do not have words to explain it or even describe it. Many times we are not fully aware the transition is even happening. It is a mysterious awakening that seems to descend on us. Depth psychologists, namely those conversant with the intricacies of our unconscious, have the same difficulties with a description of this experience and simply call it the *transcendent function.* By this, they mean we do not have to do anything other than hold still for this transcendent experience to happen. [10]As it happens, it draws us toward psychological wholeness. In the language of contemplative spirituality this gravitational force field is the dynamic of *transformation.*

Just as we use dreams to access the unconscious, slowly reading scripture stories about God and learning to move beyond the superficial, literal meanings of these stories allows us to look into our lives and change our view of who God truly is in our life. This slowly evolving process is more than simply changing our abstract concepts of God. Our movement toward a better understanding of God is itself changing our *relationship* with God. We begin to realize, for instance, if Jesus treats the shamed woman accused of adultery, with dignity and respect, so too will he treat me the same way. (John 8:53) We begin to discover there is *something* inside us that moves us toward a wider, more vulnerable openness to this mystery of God within us.

As we sit in silence, we discover a personal guidance system inside, with its own gravitational draw toward the Divine.

The Prodigal Son (Luke 15:11-32)

¹¹ Then Jesus said, "There was a man who had two sons.
¹² The younger of them said to his father, 'Father, give me the share of the property that will belong to me.' So he divided his property between them. ¹³ A few days later the younger son gathered all he had and traveled to a distant country, and there he squandered his property in dissolute living. ¹⁴ When he had spent everything, a severe famine took place throughout that country, and he began to be in need. ¹⁵ So he went and hired himself out to one of the citizens of that country, who sent him to his fields to feed the pigs. ¹⁶ He would gladly have filled himself with the pods that the pigs were eating; and no one gave him anything. ¹⁷ But when he came to himself he said, 'How many of my father's hired hands have bread enough and to spare, but here I am dying of hunger! ¹⁸ I will get up and go to my father, and I will say to him, "Father, I have sinned against heaven and before you;

¹⁹ I am no longer worthy to be called your son; treat me like one of your hired hands."' ²⁰ So he set off and went to his father. But while he was still far off, his father saw him and was filled with compassion; he ran and put his arms around him and kissed him. ²¹ Then the son said to him, 'Father, I have sinned against heaven and before you; I am no longer worthy to be called your son.' ²² But the father said to his slaves, 'Quickly, bring out a robe—the best one—and put it on him; put a ring on his finger and sandals on his feet. ²³ And get the fatted calf and kill it, and let us eat and celebrate; ²⁴ for this son of mine was dead and is alive again; he was lost and is found!' And they began to celebrate. **²⁵** "Now his elder son was in the field; and when he came and approached the house, he heard music and dancing.

²⁶ He called one of the slaves and asked what was going on. **²⁷** He replied, 'Your brother has come, and your father has killed the fatted calf, because he has got him back safe and sound.' **²⁸** Then he became angry and refused to go in. His father came out and began to plead with him. **²⁹** But he answered his father, 'Listen! For all these years I have been working like a slave for you, and I have never disobeyed your command; yet you have never given me even a young goat so that I might celebrate with my friends.

³⁰ But when this son of yours came back, who has devoured your property with prostitutes, you killed the fatted calf for him!' **³¹** Then the father said to him, 'Son, you are always with me, and all that is mine is yours. **³²** But we had to celebrate and rejoice, because this brother of yours was dead and has come to life; he was lost and has been found.'"

The slow reading of this parable, mulling over and looking carefully at the complexities of the relationships in the story, gently pulls us into a non-ordinary encounter with the mystery of God. This 'slow reading' means that we do not study the passage as if we are reading the newspaper, just skimming the story. Rather, we are to read the parable sentence by sentence, appreciating the actions and possible motives of each character and what is going on in their relationships to each other. This slow reading is trying to imagine the human motives of the characters that we can identify with. Their decisions and actions draw us into the story almost as if we are participants; as we identify with one character or another, we become aware of how this story mirrors our own.

Some background information on Luke 15:11-32 will be helpful. This is a 'parable,' a unique form of story, designed to shock listeners out of their ordinary understanding into a new way of looking at things. The original listeners would have found the behavior of the father shocking in many ways: inheritance is *never* divided before death, royalty never goes out looking for people, family and servants come to them. This father seems undisturbed by the shame falling on his family by the actions of his son. He longs for his son. His love obliterates all resentment or desire for vengeance, or even the need to "teach his son a lesson."

It is shocking for us to realize that neither son truly loved their father as he loved them but he remains undeterred by that. His own love runs so deep it can hold all their indifference and rebellion. Both sons were relating to the father in self-centered ways. They wanted something from him. As we slowly go through the parable we get drawn into our part in the story: this father loves his sons no matter what. *Is it possible that this God loves me in the same fashion, knowing that I come to him more in fear than in love?* Is this the reason Jesus is speaking this parable?

Intimacy with a Father

Jesus tells this story of the prodigal son, which is really the story of an unconditionally loving father. The parable is shocking to his listeners, forcing them to re-evaluate how they think about Yahweh, the God of their Jewish faith. This reevaluation upset and challenged the religious authorities of his day to the point that they wanted to kill him because they were afraid of how such love might override the legalistic control that kept the few in power. The parable forces us similarly to challenge our concept of God. The admonition in the Gospels to repent, is more aptly translated as think differently, or, change the way you view this, or, come at this abstract concept with a different way of 'seeing.'

This is exactly what we need to do when dealing with our experience of shame. Just as we must learn to listen to ourselves, or to another person in speaking about shame, so we must hold still, and allow ourselves to be seen by God.

An intimate relationship is not possible with a judgmental and aloof Divinity. How could we truly open up, allow ourselves to be seen at the level of our shame, if the God of our understanding cares so little about us? Healing our relationship with God, healing ourselves of shame, invites us to take another look at who this God really is. As our relationship with God is transformed into one of intimacy and trust we can allow ourselves to come out of hiding.

The admonition in the Gospels to 'repent,' is more aptly translated as 'think differently,' or, 'change the way you view this,' or, 'come at this abstract concept in a different way'.

CONCLUSION

The simple suggestion in centering prayer to let go of thoughts and detach from the stories we spin out of those thoughts, awakens the powerful emotions of shame. Our humble consent in centering prayer prepares us to address shame as a personal threat to our sense of self, not simply as a behavioral problem. The full power of simply sitting in silence, and not running away from the emotional tsunami that overtakes us, allows divine therapy to unfold. As we sit and consent to "be seen," the contemplative experience takes us deeper into the unutterable mystery of intimate relationship with God.

Those who practice contemplative prayer know by their own experience that through this receptive prayer practice, sitting and allowing God to see us, allowing the gradual purging of our unconscious experiences of a lifetime, profound healing happens. It is our personal encounter with the Ultimate Mystery whom Jesus called "Father," beyond our conscious awareness, that reaches the source of our toxic shame. We develop a place to go, a sacred space within, a true home, and a safe refuge.

Coming to terms with our unique inner life is our life's purpose. The essence of our spiritual journey is taking in our life experiences, particularly those painful and shameful images emerging from our deep unconscious, holding them, then letting the indwelling of the Spirit of God fashion us into the person we were born to be.

ENDNOTES

1. See John Bradshaw, *Healing the Shame that Binds You*, Health Communications, Ind.: 1988; and Wilkie Au and Noreen Cannon Au, *God's Unconditional Love, Healing our Shame*. Paulist Press: 2016. Many of the themes in this essay are adapted from these insightful books.

2. Throughout this essay the terms shame and toxic shame will be used interchangeably and, unless clarified, will always refer to the invisible, unconscious shame called toxic shame.

3. Van Der Kolk, M.D., *The Body Keeps the Score*, p. 211, emphasis added.

4. While centering prayer is classically defined as one form of the general notion of contemplative prayer, they are used interchangeably in this essay to describe prayer without words or concepts.

5. Personal written letter to me.

6. James Hollis, PhD, *Hauntings, Dispelling the Ghosts Who Run Our Lives*, Chiron Publications: Ashville, NC, 2013, p.76.

7. Although I use childhood trauma and toxic shame interchangeably, they are not the same. Trauma shocks the system. Toxic shame changes the way we see ourselves.

8. Epstein, *The Trauma of Everyday Life*, p. 197

9. Au, *God's Unconditional Love, Healing Our Shame*, pp 52-53.

10. Stein, *Jung's Map of the Soul*, Chicago: Open Court, pp. 144-146.

APPENDICES

A. The Easy Way to Do Centering Prayer.

Before the Prayer Time

1. There is no religious prerequisite for contemplative prayer. It is for anyone.

2. Realize that you are not trying to reach an 'empty' mind. You simply want to consent to the Divine already in your life. Your mind keeps churning with you or without you. Best you can do is not pay attention to it.

3. The best way to not pay attention is to choose a word ahead of time to remind yourself that you do not want to dwell on your thoughts. When the thoughts come, revert to the word to detach from the thought. The word itself is not important. It is not a mantra. It is simply a reminder to not attach to the thought. Words like *peace, quiet, Lord, Yahweh, God, Jesus, Allah* work well.

4. Fix a certain amount of time for the prayer. Try 20 minutes. That way, when distractions come, as they inevitably do, you will not give up until you complete the time you set. It helps to pray at a specific time each day.

The Prayer Time

5. Set your intention to let go of any 'thoughts.' These are ideas, emotions, feelings, resentments, planning that emerge as you enter your silence. This includes 'good' thoughts, even 'inspiring' or 'spiritual' thoughts. If they are important, they will surface again after prayer time. During prayer time they will hook your attention into distraction. Instead, you simply want to consent in silence to God's presence.

APPENDICES

6. Start with a few deep breaths and notice your breathing. When you do you will automatically relax and sink inward. Use your prayer word as needed or your breath if that is easier. Relax into the silence.

After the Prayer Time

7. Do not evaluate your prayer. Your prayer is without words or direct content so there is literally nothing to evaluate. Nor can you judge a good prayer time by the absence of distractions. It is your *intention* that is key to progress. After a relatively short period of time you will notice your awareness changes.

APPENDICES

B. Guidelines for Creating a Safe Group for Spiritual Journey Discussions

1. An experience of centering prayer is the key activity of the circle.

   Participants are familiar with the notions of unloading of the unconscious and more comfortable with the vulnerability experienced by moving away from our usual narratives.

2. Discussions are best *after* centering prayer.

   Immediately after a prayer period, members are in a sacred space, more conducive to deeper sharing, and more open to deeper promptings from the unconscious.

3. Real listening, without trying to prepare a response, is best.

   The more silence surrounds the discussion, the more non-ordinary the discussion becomes. Each sharing deserves its own awe and reverence before moving onto the next topic.

4. The silence of the listening creates a powerful relational space for healing.

   For many in the group listening to another share triggers associations of their own early experiences. A new perspective emerges that is the seedbed of personal healing.

5. Preserve the integrity of the group by keeping the sharing confidential.

   Talking about another's sharing, outside of the original context, can create a sense of betrayal. It betrays the original trust and dampens the likelihood of the next person's sharing.

APPENDICES

6. The freedom to remain silent is absolute.

    Forcing one to speak on this level of sharing can create a greater sense of shame and form a greater obstacle to sharing than the original experience. Privacy is essential.

7. The circle is there for support, not to give advice.

    Talking about how one 'solved' their shame issue can feel like giving advice to the one who originally shared. This usually means avoiding discussion of theology, religious doctrines, or special psychological insight.

FURTHER RESOURCES

PRISON CONTEMPLATIVE FELLOWSHIP
For a copy of Finding God Within: *Contemplative Prayer for Prisoners*, free to prisoners, and other contemplative materials to help start a centering prayer circle in your facility.
Write to:
Prison Contemplative Fellowship
P.O. Box 1086
Folsom, CA 95763-1086
USPCF. Org
Office@uspcf.org

HUMAN KINDNESS FOUNDATION
For over 50 years, HKF has responded to the spiritual needs of incarcerated people with free books, Newsletters, and personal correspondence. They serve tens of thousands of inmates in North America.
Write to:
Human Kindness Foundation
P.O. Box 61619
Durham, NC 27715
www.humankindness.org

PRISON OUTREACH
For 47 years Prison Outreach has encouraged inmates to set themselves free through meditation, mentorship, and small group work to reclaim their own divinity. Their free books and materials currently serve over 36,000 men and women in nearly 4000 prisons and jails around the world.
Write to:
The Prison Outreach Program,
Edgar Cayce's Association for
Research and Enlightenment (A.R.E.) Inc.
215 67th Street, Virginia Beach, VA 23451
EdgarCayce.org

ABOUT THE AUTHOR

Ray Leonardini practiced law for nearly thirty years. After retirement, he turned toward his foremost area of interest: The Christian spiritual journey. For the last ten years, as a volunteer chaplain, he has led meditation groups and taught contemplative prayer and the spiritual journey at Folsom State Prison and other prisons in Northern California and Oregon. He is Director of Prison Contemplative Fellowship, a nonprofit organization that sends books and prayer materials directly to prisoners and works with prison chaplains and volunteers to facilitate the startup of centering prayer groups. He is the author of *Finding God Within: Contemplative Prayer for Prisoners,* a handbook written specifically for prisoners which has been sent to more than seven hundred prisons throughout the country and is used for centering prayer groups in over one hundred prisons and jails. You can reach Ray Leonardini at *office@uspcf.org.*